Crystals a...
And this guide will help you to learn their healing powers. Often the crystals that we should choose are the ones we are most drawn to, the ones we like the look of the best!

Aegirine

This is a very high vibrational stone. It can help you with your confidence and help you to realise how strong you truly are.

Ajoite

Ajoite can help you with your worries and fears. It's also a good crystal to help you with grief. So if you have ever had a pet which has sadly died, this crystal can help you to release all of these emotions in a gentle and calm way.

Alexandrite

One of the happiest crystals you could ever own! This beautiful stone can help to bring out your happy and joyful side!

Ametrine

This crystal is also known as Bolivianite and it is a mix of Amethyst and Citrine. It can help you to be more creative, so next time you are doing an art project keep it close to you so it can help. It can also help to ease anything you are stressed about.

Ammolite

This crystal is made inside the fossilized shells of Ammonites. You can also find Calcite, Pyrite, and many other elements , so no two Ammolite crystals will ever be exactly the same. They are unique, just like you!
Keep this crystal near by if you have an exam or test to do because this stone helps with wisdom and knowledge.

Ancestralite

This crystal is very new! So there are still things to be discovered about it. This one can help ground you. Have you ever woken up and still feel likg you're dreaming? This crystal can help bring you back down to earth!

Angelite

This beautiful blue crystal can help you to connect to your angels, did you guess that from the name?

Anhydrite

This crystal can help you to release old behaviours, maybe you are trying to spend less time on your iPad or tablet, or less time watching tv? Or maybe you are trying to be a more helpful person.? Anhydrite will help you to do that.

Apatite

Apatite is amazing at helping you think of new ideas! Keep this crystal close to you, maybe in your pocket or by your bed if you need some new ideas. We think this one looks a bit like a stick of candy rock!

Apophyllite

It's crystals often look like squares. This crystal also has a high water content in it. That means it is great for conducting frequencies and can help you to reach a higher vibration. It can look a bit like a rubix cube!

Aragonite

Aragonite is a stabilising stone, which means it will make your emotions calm. It is good to hold this before meditation or when you want to be calm.

Arfvedsonite

Don't worry, we find it hard to pronounce this crystals name to haha! This crystal can help heal your throat chakra, so if you find it hard to explain yourself, or speak in front of people, this crystal can help you to do that.

Atlantisite

This is an extremely spiritual crystal and very powerful! It works to send healing vibrations from the heart, and awaken dormant energies that have been at rest for way too long.

Aura quartz

Aura quartz can help you with emotional healing, so if you have fell out with a friend for example, this crystal can help heal your emotions and make you feel better about the situation.

Auralite

This is a calming crystal. This stone helps to relax the body and can be beneficial in the removal of tension, headaches, eye strain, muscle discomfort and muscle spasms.

Azurite

This beautiful blue crystal can help you get rid of bad and worrying thoughts. Keep it near you and let all the good thoughts flow through your mind instead!

Beryl

This one is a sedative stone, that means that if you have trouble sleeping or find it hard to drift of into dream land, well, keep this crystals near your bed and it will help you to get a good nights sleep.

Bismuthinite

This crystals is great if you are feeling lonely. It can help take the feelings of loneliness away

Black lava

Did you know lava stone is also classed as a crystal? It has many healing properties due to its strong connection to the earth. One of them is that it can give you courage and strength.

Bloodstone

Bloodstone can help with circulation. The ancients use to dip it in cold water and then place it onto the body to help blood flow. Maybe that is why it is called Bloodstone?

Blue john

This crystals is found in Derbyshire in the UK. It has a calming aura bringing peace and calm into your life. It's more of a purple colour though. And it looks like a normal black rock in its natural uncut state as you can see, you would likely walk straight past it!

Blue lace agate

This is also another calming crystal! Blue lace agate is very good at healing plants to, so if you have a plant that is dying, place some into the pot with your plant, it may help it.

Bronzite

Bronzite can help restore your faith in yourself!

Brucite

Have you ever been skiing? This one can help you regulate your body temperature so it might be useful next time it snows!

Carnelian

Carnelian is very good at helping calm down anger. So next time you are mad, pick some up and keep it close to you.

Cassiterite

This one is very good for manifestation. Do you have something you really want? Tell your cassiterite crystal and it will help you to get it.

Cavansite

Cavansite can help you to express your love. So if you have someone who you want to tell, or show how much you love them, this crystal can help you to do that.

Celestine

This can help heal your throat. Next time you have a sore throat put this stone on it and see how much it helps.

Chalcopyrite

This crystal is another health healer. It's high vibration can help you to heal from a virus and help with inflammation.

Chiastolite

Do you have a test coming up soon? This crystal can help improve mental clarity, meaning it can help your brain! So if you are trying to learn and memorise something for a test, or maybe you are trying to memorise your crystals? This is a good stone to keep by you.

Chrome diopside

Chrome diopside is said to help when you have painful muscles. Try putting this crystal onto the muscle where your pain is and it will help take it away.

Chrysocolla

This crystal is known as a healing stone among Native American cultures where it has been used to strengthen the body's resistance to illness. So it can help you to not get sick. It's also a very peaceful stone.

Chrysoprase

Normally pink crystals can help to heal a broken heart as they can help heal your heart chakra, but did you know green crystals also help? Chrysoprase is very good at this.

Cordierite

Eye see! this is a crystal which can help your eye sight! Put one on your third eye, the little space between both your eyebrows and you can feel its healing powers in your eyes!

Cuprite

This one is very good at helping increase your energy. So if you ever wake up and still feel tired, maybe keep this one in your pocket to help wake you up and give you some much needed energy.

Danburite

Danburite is pure love energy! It fills you with peace and is very good at helping you get through difficult situations.

Dolomite

Dolomite can help activate your chakras. There are said to be seven chakra energy points in your body. We can not see them with our eyes, because they are invisible energy points inside you, how interesting!

Dumortierite

This one is a stone of patience. If you find it hard waiting for things then this stone can help you with that. Keep it close by next time you need some more patience.

Emerald

We often see this stone in jewelry. Do you know some people believe this stone is unlucky? But that's not true! It can help your memory and help you focus.

Eudialyte

This is a very healing stone. If you are ever physically hurt, or your feelings have been hurt, Eudialyte can help you. Look at its beautiful swirls of colour.

Faden

This one is formed between two rocks and starts very very small until over a very long time it stretches between the rocks! The slow stretching results in a string effect in quality Faden crystals, and it is said to help mend broken bones and help you get over illness quicker as it heals your aura.

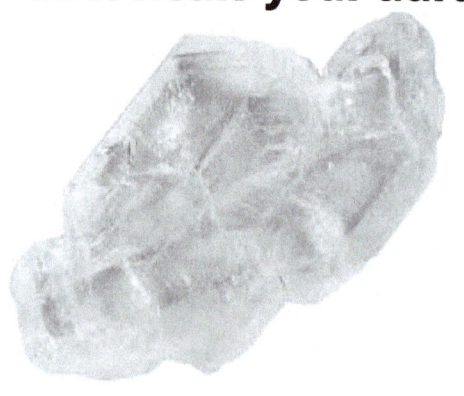

Fossilwood

This is also called petrified wood and is a fossil and also a crystal, how cool! It is said that this wood can bring you good fortune and help you to become the best version of yourself.

Fuchsite

Have you ever heard of a good luck charm? Well this is the best lucky charm you could ever have! It's high vibration can attract lots of lucky things towards you!

Gabbro

Merlin the magician, have you every heard of the legends about him? This crystal is said to hold the same magical properties Merlin had, which means it's very good for helping you practice magic!

Garnet

Garnet looks like fire and it has healing properties a bit like it. It can warm your body up and your heart!

Garnierite

This is a beautiful light green stone. It is believed it can bring lots of positivity into your life and help you attract lots of happiness! What a lovely crystal. It is also called green moonstone.

Gaspeite

Another beautiful green crystal, this one a little darker than Garnierite. This one is a grounding stone. Imagination is an amazing thing, but if you want to concentrate on your day this can help bring you back down to earth and help you focus.

Goldstone

This is a great crystal to help you with your ambitions. Have you ever really wanted to do something, like learn to play an instrument? Goldstone can help you to do that.

Goshenite

Goshenite can help you with your originality. Being yourself is an amazing thing to do. There is no one else the same as you here on earth and that is absolutely amazing and such a special thing!

Gaurdianite

This one is a protective stone. It can protect and cleanse your energy field. We swap energy all the time when we talk to our friends and family, and this crystal can help you to make sure you have enough, and make sure you do not feel to tired after a day of talking to lots of people!

Hackmanite

This crystal is good for a lot of things! It can help with pretty much everything and is good to keep around your other crystals to make them even more powerful.

Healerite

Healerite is very good for your nervous system. This means if you are ever nervous or worried about something, if you keep it near you, it can help you to feel a lot more calm and your nerves can melt away!

Healers gold

Found recently in the desert of Arizona, wow! It is also a heavy crystal. It can help you have a happy flow of energy through your chakras.

Heliodor

The yellow that is in Helidor is from the Iron that the crystal has inside it. Some people call this crystal the healing light, and it can help to heal you heart and many other things.

Hematite

Hematite can help you from absorbing other peoples energy. So if you are are ever around someone who puts you into a bad mood sometimes, keep Hematite by you to help keep their energy away.

Hemimorphite

This one can give you heightened Awareness and Intuition. Have you ever thought about a friend and then they have suddenly knocked on the door or called you? That was your intuition telling you that they was about to call around.

Herkimer diamond

Although it's name suggests it is a diamond, it is in fact not, and is acctually a variety of quartz. It gets the name diamond from its clear clarity (It looks just like a diamond). They can help cleanse you and get rid of polution and toxins.

Hiddenite

This is a very good crystal for helping you to manifest things! So if there is something you really want, maybe a new game or a new bike, concentrate and feel the feelings you would have as if you really did already have it, and know that it is already on its way, and with hiddenite's help it might just come that much quicker!

Hilutite

Hilutite is good for helping you to see the positive side of life. So in other words, it can help you to become a happier person and to find joy in every day!

ilvaite

Have you ever had an adult say to you "patience is a virtue", well, next time they say that to you, ask them to buy you this crystal! Because it can help you to have better patience.

iolite

Iolite can assist in healing of the eyes, migraines and headaches, disorientation and dizziness. It can also help improve your memory. Place it on your forehead next time you have a headache.

isua stone

Isua Stone is highly protective. Think of it like a guard dog to your energy. It wont let anyone else's negative energy effect yours!

Jade

Jade can help support the kidneys and the urinary tract (that's where you wee from!) It is sometimes referred to as the "spleen stone" because of its benefits to this organ also.

Jet

Jet is another protective stone (most dark crystals have that same quality about them). It is very good at helping with past also. It can help ease anxiety, sadness and any loss you may of had.

K2 stone

K2 is an extremely spiritual stone. It can help you to lucid dream, which means it can help you to have those dreams where you are aware you are actually asleep and dreaming, so you can control them, I like to go flying in mine. What about you, have you had a lucid dream before?

Kammererite

This crystal has a very beautiful energy! It is great to use in meditation. Like K2 stone, it is also a very spiritual stone and can help open your third eye.

Kunzite

Kunzite is a very sweet and loving crystal. It can help to open up your heart. It can help you to generate loving and kind thoughts.

Kyanite

Kyanite is a very calming stone. It can help heal your throat chakra and can also help you to communicate what you want to say in a positive way.

Lakelandite

Lakelandite is thought to be beneficial when treating the kidneys, spleen and stomach. It is also believed to help with skin complaints and with treating disorders of the reproductive system.

Larimar

Larimar is an earth-healing stone. It connects with nature and will counteract imbalances in the earth's energy. It can also help you to find inner wisom.

Lavakite

This one is a beautiful collection of high energy vibrations. Larvikite aids in the recovery of strokes and helps brain function. It cleanses and purifies body tissue, harmonises the metabolism and helps with muscular detoxification.

Lepidolite

Lepidolite is a balancing stone. It can help to calm your mind and see situations from both sides. It's good to hold if you are not sure about something. It can help you come to a good informed decision.

Chakras

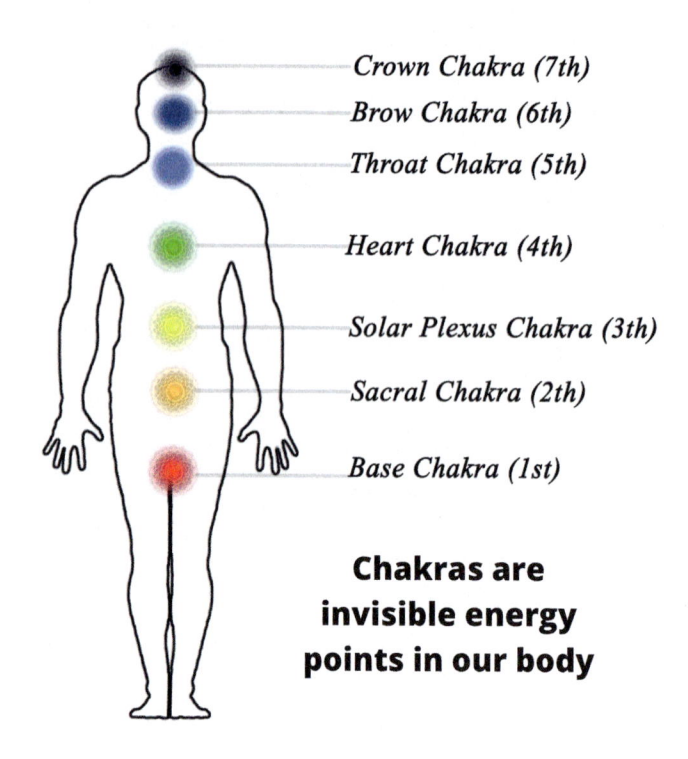

- Crown Chakra (7th)
- Brow Chakra (6th)
- Throat Chakra (5th)
- Heart Chakra (4th)
- Solar Plexus Chakra (3th)
- Sacral Chakra (2th)
- Base Chakra (1st)

Chakras are invisible energy points in our body

Printed in Great Britain
by Amazon